A TRUE BOOK™

My United States
Nebraska

JENNIFER ZEIGER

Children's Press®
An Imprint of Scholastic Inc.

Content Consultant
James Wolfinger, PhD, Associate Dean and Professor
College of Education, DePaul University, Chicago, Illinois

Library of Congress Cataloging-in-Publication Data
Names: Zeiger, Jennifer, author.
Title: Nebraska / by Jennifer Zeiger.
Description: New York : Children's Press, [2018] | Series: A true book | Includes bibliographical references
    and index.
Identifiers: LCCN 2018014923 | ISBN 9780531235645 (library binding) | ISBN 9780531250839 (pbk.)
Subjects: LCSH: Nebraska—Juvenile literature.
Classification: LCC F666.3 .Z45 2018 | DDC 978.2—dc23
LC record available at https://lccn.loc.gov/2018014923

Photographs ©: cover: Walter Bibikow/Getty Images; back cover bottom: Walter Bibikow/AWL Images; back cover ribbon: AliceLiddelle/
Getty Images; 3 bottom: Radharc Images/Alamy Images; 3 map: Jim McMahon/Mapman ®; 4 left: Scisetti Alfio/Shutterstock; 4 right:
J M Barres/age fotostock; 5 bottom: Lidia fotografie/Shutterstock; 5 top: Christian Heeb/Getty Images; 6 bottom: Nebraska Tourism;
7 bottom: Walter Bibikow/Getty Images; 7 center: Nebraska Tourism; 7 top: Matthew J Brand/Shutterstock; 8-9: Peter Haigh/Alamy
Images; 11: Nebraska Tourism; 12: marekuliasz/Shutterstock; 13: Gene Rhoden/Weatherpix/Getty Images; 14: Tom Till/Superstock,
Inc.; 15: Krisztian Farkas/Shutterstock; 16-17: Stephen Saks Photography/Alamy Images; 19: Todd Bannor/Alamy Images; 20: Tigatelu/
Dreamstime; 22 left: BigAlBaloo/Shutterstock; 22 right: grebeshkovmaxim/Shutterstock; 23 top right: Scisetti Alfio/Shutterstock; 23
center right: Lidia fotografie/Shutterstock; 23 bottom right: J M Barres/age fotostock; 23 top left: Daniel Prudek/Shutterstock; 23 center
left: StevenRussellSmithPhotos/Shutterstock; 23 bottom left: beverlyjane/Shutterstock; 24-25: ZUMA Press, Inc./Alamy Images; 27: Peter
Newark American Pictures/Bridgeman Images; 29: The Granger Collection; 30 top: Peter Newark American Pictures/Bridgeman Images;
30 bottom: MPI/Getty Images; 31 bottom: North Wind Picture Archives/Alamy Images; 31 top left: BigAlBaloo/Shutterstock; 31 top right:
Weldon Schloneger/Shutterstock; 32: Historical/Getty Images; 33: Paul Fearn/Alamy Images; 34-35: Christian Heeb/Getty Images; 36:
Icon Sports Wire/Getty Images; 37: Nebraska Tourism; 38: Weldon Schloneger/Shutterstock; 39: Andrew Linscott/Alamy Images; 40
inset: Corben_D/iStockphoto; 40 background: PepitoPhotos/Getty Images; 41: Nebraska Tourism; 42 top left: Album/Newscom; 42 top
right: David Hume Kennerly/Getty Images; 42 bottom left: Photo 12/Alamy Images; 42 center: Library of Congress; 42 bottom right:
Kristoffer Tripplaar/Alamy Images; 43 top left: Gisela Schober/Getty Images; 43 top right: David Livingston/Getty Images; 43 bottom left:
Gabriel Olsen/Getty Images; 43 bottom center: Scott Dudelson/Getty Images; 43 bottom right: Imagesport/Newscom; 43 center right:
Aspenphoto/Dreamstime; 43 center left: Carrienelson1/Dreamstime; 44 top: Brent Hofacker/Alamy Images; 44 bottom: Ammodramus/
Wikimedia; 44 center: Tom Till/Superstock, Inc.; 45 bottom: MPI/Getty Images; 45 top right: Steven Branscombe/Getty Images; 45 top left:
Peter Haigh/Alamy Images.

Maps by Map Hero, Inc.

Front cover: Scotts Bluff

**Back cover: Strategic Air Command
& Aerospace Museum**

Welcome to Nebraska

Find the Truth!

Everything you are about to read is true *except* for one of the sentences on this page.

Which one is **TRUE**?

T or F Nebraska was once part of an area of land called Louisiana.

T or F The weather in Nebraska is hot all year long.

Find the answers in this book.

Key Facts

Capital: Lincoln

Estimated population as of 2017: 1,920,076

Nickname: Cornhusker State

Biggest cities: Omaha, Lincoln, Grand Island

UNITED STATES

Nebraska

NEBRASKA
RVX 044
2011 • nebraska.gov

Contents

THE BIG TRUTH!

Blue chalcedony

What Represents Nebraska?

Goldenrod

Carhenge

3 History

How did Nebraska become
the state it is today? **25**

4 Culture

What do Nebraskans do for work and fun? **35**

Western
meadowlark

This Is Nebraska!

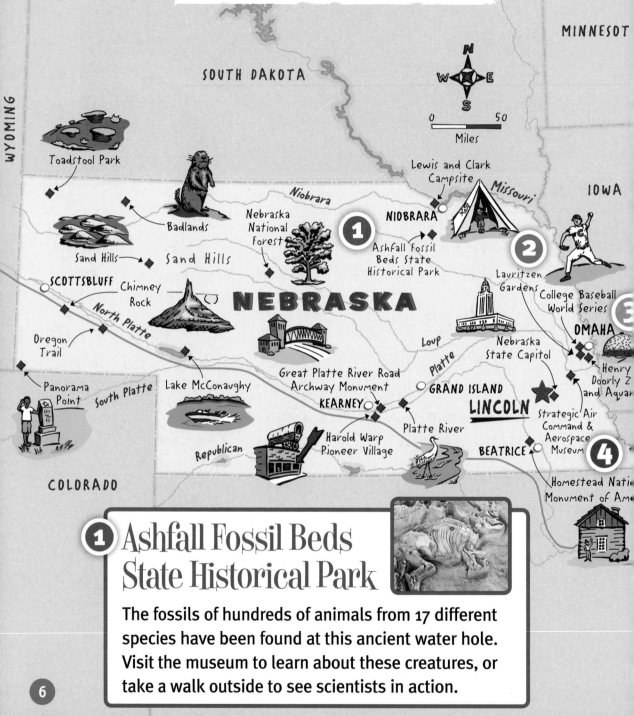

MINNESOT

SOUTH DAKOTA

WYOMING

IOWA

Toadstool Park

Badlands

Niobrara

Nebraska National Forest

Lewis and Clark Campsite

Missouri

NIOBRARA

1 Ashfall Fossil Beds State Historical Park

Sand Hills

Sand Hills

SCOTTSBLUFF

Chimney Rock

2

Lauritzen Gardens

College Baseball World Series

3

OMAHA

Oregon Trail

North Platte

NEBRASKA

Loup

Nebraska State Capitol

Henry Doorly Z and Aquar

Panorama Point

South Platte

Lake McConaughy

Platte

GRAND ISLAND

LINCOLN

Great Platte River Road Archway Monument

KEARNEY

Platte River

Strategic Air Command & Aerospace Museum

4

Republican

Harold Warp Pioneer Village

BEATRICE

COLORADO

Homestead Nati Monument of Am

0   50
Miles

1 Ashfall Fossil Beds State Historical Park

The fossils of hundreds of animals from 17 different species have been found at this ancient water hole. Visit the museum to learn about these creatures, or take a walk outside to see scientists in action.

❷ Lauritzen Gardens

Located in downtown Omaha, these gardens offer a living, growing exploration of plant life year-round. Come to learn or just take a break surrounded by peace and nature.

❸ Henry Doorly Zoo and Aquarium

Explore a world of wildlife in this Omaha attraction, featuring animals from deserts, jungles, deep oceans, and blue skies. If you don't feel like walking, view the zoo from above on the Skyfari or travel through it on a train or tram.

❹ Strategic Air Command & Aerospace Museum

From war planes to spacecraft, this museum in Ashland offers a look at the science of flight. Special flight simulators even make you feel like you're the pilot in the cockpit!

Nebraska covers 76,824 square miles (198,973 square kilometers) of land.

CHAPTER 1

Land and Wildlife

Looking out over the landscape of Nebraska, the first thing you might notice is how flat everything looks. There are no mountain ranges and few tall trees. Big cities are few and far between. But Nebraska has plenty to see. It is a land of sprawling farms, rolling hills, and even the occasional rock formation.

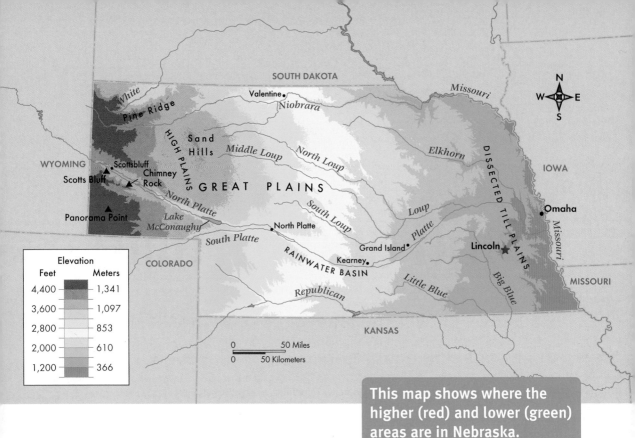

This map shows where the higher (red) and lower (green) areas are in Nebraska.

Low and Rolling

Nebraska is part of a region called the Great Plains. This huge area of grassland stretches across the western United States from Canada in the north nearly all the way south to Mexico. The Sand Hills are in north-central Nebraska. As their name suggests, they are hills of sand, or dunes. This area is dotted with lakes, ponds, and marshes.

Chimney Rock towers about 300 feet (91 meters) above the surrounding land.

Remarkable Rocks

The dunes of the Sand Hills are prevented from blowing away by the grass that grows on them. The western part of Nebraska is sometimes called the panhandle. This land is home to several steep, towering rock formations, such as Scotts Bluff and Chimney Rock. It also features an area called Toadstool Geological Park. Here, hundreds of unusual, mushroom-shaped rocks rise up from the ground. Stripes in the rocks show how different layers formed over millions of years. There are also many ancient animal **fossils** in the park.

The Dismal River winds for about 72 miles (116 kilometers) through the Sand Hills.

Flowing Rivers

Most of Nebraska's towns and cities are located along the state's rivers. The Missouri and Platte Rivers are the state's main waterways. The Missouri River forms the eastern border of the state. The Platte is a steady, shallow river that runs eastward across the state until it meets the Missouri. The two rivers join together just south of Omaha, Nebraska's largest city.

Hot and Cold

Nebraskans are used to a wide range of weather conditions. Summers can be very hot, and winters are often very cold. Throughout the state, weather conditions can shift suddenly, with pleasant weather one day giving way to storms or extreme temperatures the next. Thunderstorms and tornadoes are common in spring and summer, while blizzards often blanket the state in snow in winter.

More than 100 tornadoes can hit Nebraska in a single year.

MAXIMUM TEMPERATURE 118°F

MINIMUM TEMPERATURE -47°F

Growing in Nebraska

Farmland covers most of Nebraska. This means crops such as corn, soybeans, and wheat are some of the state's most common plants. Plenty of wild plants grow in Nebraska, too. A variety of grasses grow in the state's prairies and in the Sand Hills. Nebraska doesn't have much forestland. Trees such as cedar and pine cover only about 3 percent of the state.

At Ponca State Park in northeastern Nebraska, it is possible to look across the Missouri River into both Iowa and South Dakota at the same time.

Nebraska's Wild Animals

Many different animal species can be found in Nebraska. Deer, coyotes, beavers, turkeys, prairie dogs, and rabbits are all common. The state's rockier areas are home to

Prairie dogs dig underground burrows with complex systems of tunnels and rooms.

bighorn sheep. Several **endangered** species live in Nebraska. Among them are the black-footed ferret and the piping plover. Perhaps the most well-known animal in Nebraska is the sandhill crane. About 500,000 cranes travel to the state each spring as part of their yearly **migration**. Their arrival draws bird watchers from around the world to the banks of the Platte River.

The statues and other artwork inside Nebraska's capitol pay tribute to the state's Native American and pioneer history.

JOHNSON SHERIDAN WEBSTER FILLMORE NUCKOLLS KEARNEY KNOX RED WILLOW

CHAPTER 2

Government

During Nebraska's time as a **territory**, its capital was located in Omaha. But when Nebraska became a state in 1867, the people chose to move their center of government to a new city. They named it Lincoln, after President Abraham Lincoln, who had died just two years before. The first two capitols built there were not well-constructed and eventually became unusable. But the third—and current—capitol was built to stand the test of time.

Three Branches

Nebraska's government is organized into three branches. The executive branch makes sure state laws are carried out. It is led by the governor along with a number of other officials. The judicial branch oversees trials and determines punishments for crimes. The legislative branch writes the state's laws.

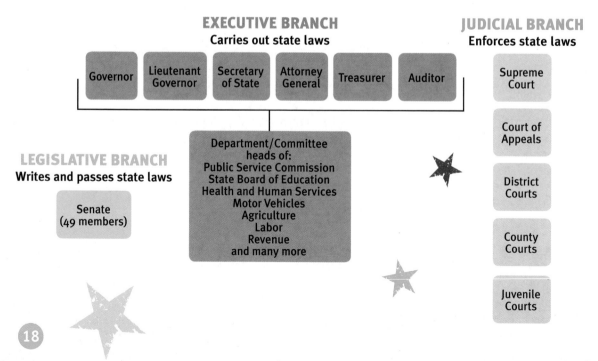

NEBRASKA'S STATE GOVERNMENT

EXECUTIVE BRANCH
Carries out state laws

Governor	Lieutenant Governor	Secretary of State	Attorney General	Treasurer	Auditor

Department/Committee heads of:
Public Service Commission
State Board of Education
Health and Human Services
Motor Vehicles
Agriculture
Labor
Revenue
and many more

JUDICIAL BRANCH
Enforces state laws

Supreme Court

Court of Appeals

District Courts

County Courts

Juvenile Courts

LEGISLATIVE BRANCH
Writes and passes state laws

Senate
(49 members)

A Unique Legislature

Most states and the U.S. government have two houses in their legislature: a senate and a house of representatives. Nebraska has only one house, called the Nebraska Unicameral. It's the only state in the country with one legislative house.

Nebraska is also special because its legislative members, called senators, do not belong to **political parties**. Nearly all U.S. politicians belong to either the Democratic Party or the Republican Party. Nebraska state senators are the exception.

Nebraska in the National Government

Each state elects officials to represent it in the U.S. Congress. Like every state, Nebraska has two senators. The U.S. House of Representatives relies on a state's population to determine its numbers. Nebraska has three representatives in the House.

Every four years, states vote on the next U.S. president. Each state is granted a number of electoral votes based on its number of members in Congress. With two senators and three representatives, Nebraska has five electoral votes.

2 senators and 3 representatives

5 electoral votes

With five electoral votes, Nebraska's voice in presidential elections is below average compared to other states.

The People of Nebraska

Elected officials in Nebraska represent a population with a range of interests, lifestyles, and backgrounds.

Ethnicity (2016 estimates)

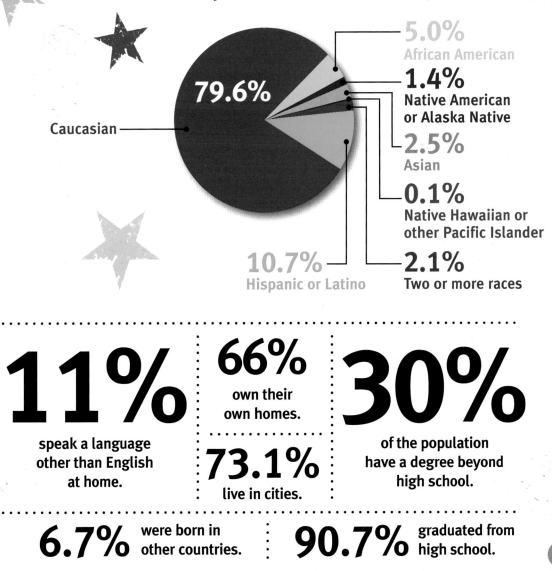

79.6%
Caucasian

5.0%
African American

1.4%
Native American or Alaska Native

2.5%
Asian

0.1%
Native Hawaiian or other Pacific Islander

2.1%
Two or more races

10.7%
Hispanic or Latino

11% speak a language other than English at home.

66% own their own homes.

73.1% live in cities.

30% of the population have a degree beyond high school.

6.7% were born in other countries.

90.7% graduated from high school.

What Represents Nebraska?

States choose specific animals, plants, and objects to represent the values and characteristics of the land and its people. Find out why these symbols were chosen to represent Nebraska or discover surprising curiosities about them.

Seal

The state seal was chosen in June 1867, shortly after Nebraska became a state. It features many symbols of Nebraska's history and economy, including a blacksmith shaping metal with a hammer and anvil, a field of crops, and a speeding train.

Flag

Nebraska's state flag simply displays the state seal against a dark-blue field. The flag was adopted in 1925, making it the final state to choose a flag design until Alaska and Hawaii became states 34 years later.

Honeybee
STATE INSECT
Honeybees play an important role in pollinating many of Nebraska's crops and wild plants.

Goldenrod
STATE FLOWER
This bright-yellow wildflower grows throughout Nebraska in fields and meadows.

Channel Catfish
STATE FISH
Many Nebraskans enjoy fishing for channel catfish in the state's rivers and lakes.

Western Meadowlark
STATE BIRD
This yellow-breasted bird lives throughout the state and is famous for its unique song.

Little Bluestem
STATE GRASS
Also known as beard grass, this plant grows wild in much of the Great Plains.

Blue Chalcedony
STATE GEMSTONE
Found in northwestern Nebraska, this gem—commonly called blue agate—is often used to make jewelry.

For more than 150 years, Native Americans from around the country have come to Nebraska each summer for the Winnebago Homecoming Celebration & Powwow.

CHAPTER 3

History

Humans first arrived in Nebraska about 12,000 years ago. They came in search of mammoths, huge ground sloths, bison, and other animals. These early Nebraskans were **nomads** who hunted using handmade spears with wooden handles and stone tips. Over thousands of years, people began settling down, forming villages, and raising crops. But sometime around 1400 CE, Nebraska's people began leaving the area for reasons no one knows today.

Native Nebraskans

In the 1500s, new groups of people began moving to Nebraska, replacing those who had left. Among them were the Pawnee, Omaha, Oto, and Ponca. Nebraska's Native American people spent most of their time in permanent villages and raised crops such as corn. They also went on long hunting trips. During these trips, they followed herds of bison and other animals. Along the way, they slept in portable homes called tipis.

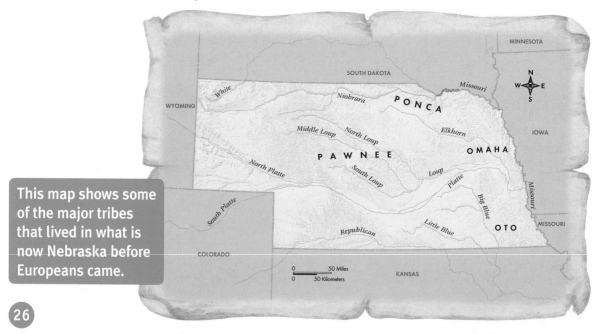

This map shows some of the major tribes that lived in what is now Nebraska before Europeans came.

Horses allowed Native Americans to chase down animals such as bison and fire arrows at them.

A New Way to Travel

When you imagine the American West, you might picture wild horses, cowboys, and Native Americans hunting on horseback. But horses are not native to the continent. Spanish conquerors and **colonizers** brought them to North America beginning in the 1500s. By the 1700s, many Native Americans in the plains were using horses. This allowed them to travel farther and faster. Hunting large herd animals such as bison became easier. Interacting with other Native American groups also became simpler and more common.

Changes in Ownership

Settlers from Spain, France, and Great Britain spent much of the 16th and 17th centuries dividing North America among themselves. The land that is now Nebraska was part of a large area that spent time as both French and Spanish territories. The Europeans didn't explore much of this land, however. In 1803, France sold the entire area, called Louisiana, to the United States.

This map shows routes Europeans took as they explored and settled what is now Nebraska.

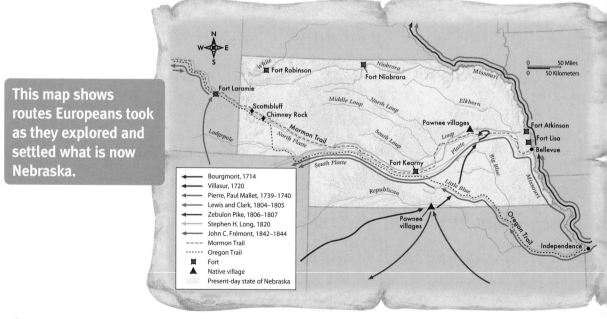

Lewis and Clark relied on the guidance of a Shoshone woman named Sacagawea as they journeyed through the Louisiana Territory.

On the Way Out West

In 1804, Meriwether Lewis and William Clark explored eastern Nebraska during their expedition to the Louisiana Territory. During the early 1800s, fur traders, trappers, and other travelers moved across Nebraska. Most people passed through on their way west along the Oregon Trail and other routes. So many people crossed Nebraska that their wagons left deep tracks in the ground. In parts of Nebraska, these tracks still remain.

Becoming Nebraska

Nebraska officially became a separate territory in 1854. More settlers began to stop in Nebraska instead of continuing west, and the U.S. government began forcing Nebraska's Native Americans onto **reservations**. Nebraska became an important agricultural center. It also remained a travel hub. In 1865, construction began on a transcontinental railroad connecting Omaha and California.

Timeline of Nebraska Events

10,000 BCE
People arrive in Nebraska for the first time.

1803
The United States obtains Nebraska as part of the Louisiana Purchase.

10,000 BCE	1500 CE	1803	1854

1500 CE
New cultures such as the Pawnee, Omaha, Oto, and Ponca begin moving into Nebraska.

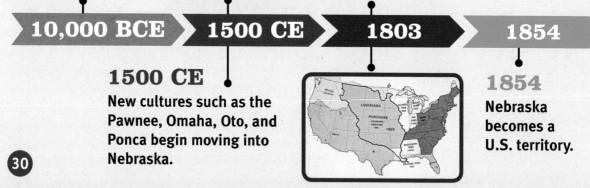

1854
Nebraska becomes a U.S. territory.

With its population growing, Nebraska was ready to become a state. After creating a government and a constitution, Nebraska was officially approved as the 37th state in 1867. In the following decades, Nebraska's farm economy faced many setbacks from problems such as **droughts** and grasshopper swarms. Conditions improved as farmers began to adopt new farming methods to protect the land.

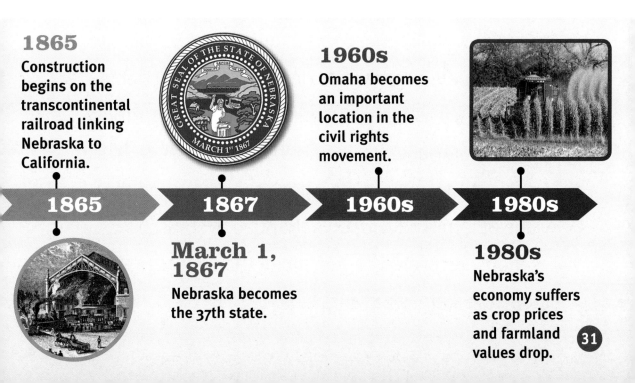

1865
Construction begins on the transcontinental railroad linking Nebraska to California.

1960s
Omaha becomes an important location in the civil rights movement.

1865 · 1867 · 1960s · 1980s

March 1, 1867
Nebraska becomes the 37th state.

1980s
Nebraska's economy suffers as crop prices and farmland values drop.

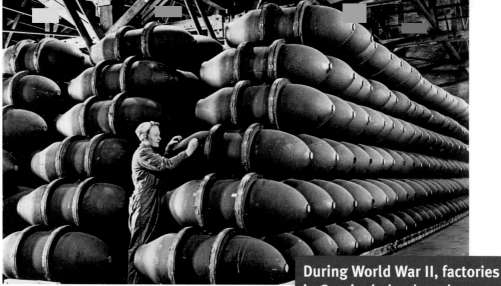

During World War II, factories in Omaha helped produce weapons and other important military supplies.

Modern Nebraska

After World War II (1939–1945), the U.S. Strategic Air Command was headquartered near Omaha, providing many jobs. Business boomed for Nebraska's railroad and agriculture companies. In the 1960s, civil rights leaders such as Ernest Chambers and Mildred Brown fought for racial equality in Nebraska. The state faced a crisis in the early 1980s when crop prices and the value of farmland suddenly dropped. Nebraska's economy recovered by the end of the decade, and today the state is thriving.

Writing Nebraska

The writings of Willa Cather (1873–1947) brought the beauty and struggle of Nebraska prairie life to the rest of the nation. Cather's family moved from Virginia to Nebraska in 1883. There, Cather was surrounded by **immigrants** from Sweden, Germany, and elsewhere. These were the pioneers who turned the wild prairie into farmland. When Cather later began writing novels, her childhood among the pioneers inspired such works as *O Pioneers!* and *My Ántonia*. Decades after their publication, these novels remain an important part of Nebraska's history and identity.

In 1923, Cather won the Pulitzer Prize for her novel *One of Ours*.

The town of Alliance is home to a site where 39 cars are stacked up to resemble the famous rock structures of Stonehenge in England. This attraction is known as Carhenge.

CHAPTER 4

Culture

Nebraska is home to a vibrant culture. The state's artists have influenced not only fellow Nebraskans but also people around the world. Hollywood actors such as Marlon Brando and Henry Fonda and rock musicians such as the members of Bright Eyes and Cursive are Nebraska natives. Museums across the state display works from both Nebraskans and other U.S. and international artists. Cowboys test their skills at the state's many rodeo events.

Sports and Recreation

Nebraskans are die-hard sports fans. Football season brings out the bright-red flags with the large "N" for the University of Nebraska–Lincoln Cornhuskers. The school also has successful basketball and other sports teams. In spring, the best teams in college baseball come to Omaha

to compete in the College World Series. Swimmers visit Omaha to try out for the U.S. Olympic team, and ice-skaters compete there in national championships.

A player charges toward the basket during a Cornhuskers game in 2016.

Nebraska Celebrations

Arbor Day began in Nebraska in 1872. Since then, millions of trees have been planted in Nebraska and around the world each April. The state's biggest Arbor Day celebration takes place in Nebraska City. Kearney is home to the largest

At the Arbor Day Farm in Nebraska City, visitors can climb tall trees using ropes.

gathering of sandhill cranes in the world. The yearly Nebraska Crane Festival brings in speakers, activities, and bird-watching groups. Art fans visit the Omaha Summer Arts Festival to check out local artists, food stands, and music stages.

Farmers use machines called combines to cut down grain crops and separate the grain from the rest of the plant all at once.

Nebraskans at Work

More Nebraskans work in services than in any other type of job. Insurance companies and tourism are major parts of Nebraska's service industry. Farms no longer employ as many Nebraskans as they once did, but they are still a major part of the state's economy. The state's main crops include corn, wheat, and soybeans. Cattle, pigs, chickens, and sheep are raised on ranches. Factories are also an important part of Nebraska's economy. Many of them create products from the meat and grains produced by the state's farmers.

Changing Corn

Corn has long been an important food crop. In addition to being a tasty side dish, it is used to feed livestock and create pet food. But believe it or not, this incredible crop can also be used to power vehicles. Today, many Nebraska farmers grow corn that is used to produce a fuel called ethanol. Ethanol is then blended with regular gasoline and pumped into cars and other vehicles all around the country. More than 30 percent of all the corn produced in Nebraska today is used to create fuel.

After its role in producing ethanol is fulfilled, the used corn can be turned into food for farm animals.

Time to Eat

The foods grown and raised in Nebraska all have a place on the state's dinner tables. Beef might be grilled on a sunny day. Or it might be ground, mixed with onions and cabbage, and baked inside a soft bread roll. This delicious sandwich, invented in Nebraska, is called a runza. Corn is another local favorite, whether served buttered on the cob or baked into cornbread.

Cornbread

Ask an adult to help you!

Serve this tasty treat alongside a bowl of chili or enjoy it by itself!

Ingredients
1 cup flour
$1/4$ cup sugar
$1/2$ teaspoon salt
3 teaspoons baking powder

1 cup yellow cornmeal
$1/4$ cup shortening
1 cup milk
1 egg, beaten

Directions
Preheat the oven to 425° F. In a small bowl, mix the flour, sugar, salt, baking powder, and cornmeal. In a large bowl, mix the shortening, milk, and egg. Stir in the dry ingredients. Beat the mixture for about a minute. Pour into a greased 8-inch-square baking pan. Bake for 20 to 25 minutes. Set on a rack to cool. Cut into 2-inch squares and enjoy!

Nebraska's fields and farms are packed with fun things to do.

A Lot to Love

From dramatic rock formations and rushing river waters to the bright lights and crowds of Omaha, there is something for everyone in Nebraska. Born-and-raised Nebraskans and first-time tourists alike love the state for its natural beauty, laid-back culture, and rich history. Taste the local cuisine, enjoy some Nebraska art, and soak up everything this incredible state has to offer! ★

Famous People

Fred Astaire

(1899–1987) was a dancer, singer, and actor who appeared in many movies, TV shows, and Broadway musicals. He was an Omaha native.

Gerald Ford

(1913–2006) served as the 38th president of the United States from 1974 to 1977. He was born in Omaha.

Marlon Brando

(1924–2004) was an award-winning actor who appeared in such classic films as *The Godfather*, *On the Waterfront*, and *A Streetcar Named Desire*. He was from Omaha.

Malcolm X

(1925–1965) was a minister and activist who fought for the rights of black people during the civil rights movement. He was born in Omaha.

Warren Buffett

(1930–) is an investor and businessman who is one of the wealthiest people in the world. He is a lifelong resident of Omaha, which also serves as the headquarters of his company, Berkshire Hathaway.

Nicholas Sparks

(1965–) is the best-selling author of novels such as *The Notebook* and *A Walk to Remember*. He is from Omaha.

Hilary Swank

(1974–) is an Academy Award–winning actor who has starred in such films as *Million Dollar Baby* and *Boys Don't Cry*. She was born in Lincoln.

Gabrielle Union

(1972–) is an actor who has appeared in such films as *She's All That* and *Bring It On*. She was born in Omaha.

Joba Chamberlain

(1985–) is a retired Major League Baseball pitcher. He grew up in Lincoln and attended the University of Nebraska.

Roxane Gay

(1974–) is an author and professor who has written novels, short stories, essays, and comic books. She was born in Omaha and attended the University of Nebraska–Lincoln.

Conor Oberst

(1980–) is a singer, songwriter, and musician who performs as a solo artist and with bands such as Bright Eyes and Desaparecidos. He was born and raised in Omaha.

Andy Roddick

(1982–) is a retired pro tennis star who was once ranked the number one player in the world. He was born in Omaha.

Did You Know That ...

Omaha is widely believed to be the birthplace of the famous Reuben sandwich, a delicious combination of corned beef, sauerkraut, Swiss cheese, and Thousand Island dressing served warm on rye bread. The sandwich is said to have been named for a local grocer named Reuben Kulakofsky.

The state's highest point is Panorama Point, which rises to 5,424 feet (1,653 m) in western Nebraska. It is not a hill, but an area of flat plains. A stone marker (pictured) identifies the highest point.

The name *Nebraska* comes from the Oto word *Nebrathka*, which means "flat water." This was the Oto name for the Platte River.

On Cornhuskers game days, more than 85,000 fans pack into Memorial Stadium in Lincoln. That means the entire population of any town in Nebraska except for Omaha or Lincoln could fit into the stadium!

Nearly 75 percent of Nebraskans live in about 1 percent of the state's land. This means much of the state is sparsely populated.

Did you find the truth?

T Nebraska was once part of an area of land called Louisiana.

F The weather in Nebraska is hot all year long.

Resources

Books

Bailer, Darice. *What's Great About Nebraska?* Minneapolis: Lerner Publications, 2015.

Cather, Willa. *O Pioneers!* Boston: Houghton Mifflin, 1913.

Heinrichs, Ann. *Nebraska.* New York: Children's Press, 2014.

Rozett, Louise (ed.). *Fast Facts About the 50 States: Plus Puerto Rico and Washington, D.C.* New York: Children's Press, 2010.

Visit this Scholastic website for more information on Nebraska:

★ www.factsfornow.scholastic.com
Enter the keyword **Nebraska**

Important Words

colonizers (KAH-luh-nye-zurz) people who leave their country to settle and take control over a new area

droughts (DROUTS) long periods without rain

endangered (en-DAYN-jurd) in danger of becoming extinct, usually because of human activity

fossils (FAH-suhlz) bones, shells, or other traces of animals or plants from millions of years ago, preserved as rock

immigrants (IM-ih-gruhnts) people who move from one country to another and settle there

migration (mye-GRAY-shuhn) movement of people or animals from one region or habitat to another

nomads (NOH-madz) members of a community that travels from place to place instead of living in the same place all the time

political parties (puh-LIT-ih-kuhl PAHR-teez) organized groups of people with similar political beliefs who sponsor candidates in elections

reservations (rez-ur-VAY-shuhnz) areas of land set aside by the government for a special purpose, such as creating a specific place where Native Americans are allowed to live

territory (TER-ih-tor-ee) an area connected with or owned by a country that is outside the country's main borders

Index

Page numbers in **bold** indicate illustrations.

About the Author

Jennifer Zeiger was born and raised in Missouri. In fact, she grew up in Hannibal, the same childhood home as Mark Twain. Her favorite part of living there was exploring the caves. Today, she lives in Chicago, Illinois, where she writes and edits kids' books.